Collins
MUSIC

How to teach
Composition
in the secondary classroom

50
INSPIRING IDEAS

Rachel Shapey

William Collins' dream of knowledge for all began with the publication of his first book in 1819.
A self-educated mill worker, he not only enriched millions of lives, but also founded a flourishing publishing house. Today, staying true to this spirit, Collins books are packed with inspiration, innovation and practical expertise. They place you at the centre of a world of possibility and give you exactly what you need to explore it. Collins. Freedom to teach.

An imprint of HarperCollins*Publishers*
The News Building
1 London Bridge Street
London
SE1 9GF

HarperCollins*Publishers*
Macken House
39/40 Mayor Street Upper
Dublin 1
D01 C9W8
Ireland

www.collins.co.uk

10 9 8 7 6 5

ISBN 978-0-00-841290-6

British Library Cataloguing in Publication Data
A catalogue record for this publication is available from the British Library.

Author: Rachel Shapey
Commissioning editor: Naomi Cook
Development editor: Em Wilson
Proofreader: Ann Barkway
Cover designer: Angela English
Internal designer: Ken Vail Graphic Design
Production controller: Lyndsey Rogers
Printed and bound by Ashford Colour Ltd.

MIX
Paper
FSC™ C007454

Acknowledgements

I would like to thank the following people for their contribution towards the writing of this book: my parents and secondary school music teachers, who encouraged me to perform and compose and pursue a career in music; Professor Martin Fautley, during my PGCE year and beyond, for inspiring me to always teach musically; everyone who has supported *I Can Compose*; finally, my husband, Iestyn, for his unwavering support and encouragement.

Table of contents

Approach by style and genre

Composing techniques

Teaching approaches

To access the online resources mentioned throughout the book, visit:
collins.co.uk/teachcomposition/download

Introduction

There is no right or wrong way to teach composing. What works for one teacher and set of students may not work for another teacher with a different class. This book has been written to offer a range of starting points, activities and advice for secondary teachers at any stage of their careers. All the ideas and approaches have been tried and tested in the classroom and are presented here for you to adapt and develop in your own music department.

Teaching composition can be challenging for a number of reasons – perhaps you weren't taught to compose yourself and consequently don't feel confident teaching it; your school may lack equipment and resources; you might feel baffled by the examination coursework marking criteria; the music curriculum (perhaps beyond your control) may not place value on composing; music is on a 'carousel' for KS3 and time is very limited… the list goes on! Whatever the reasons, there is always scope for students to compose in some capacity and for everyone to experience the joy of the creative process.

Listening to a wide range of composers and styles is hugely important when composing and will be referred to many times throughout the book. The concise nature of the book format means there isn't space to offer listening for all ideas, so the additional content online includes a listening table as well as other resources to accompany and enhance the material.

In 2019, *Sound and Music* commissioned a national survey to find out how much composition was being taught in the UK and what support and provision there was for educators. The findings from the *#CanCompose: National Music Educators Survey* revealed that there are insufficient opportunities for young people to compose and a lack of composing-specific CPD for less-experienced teachers. The findings from this survey can be read here: **soundandmusic.org/our-impact/can-compose**

Despite this somewhat negative picture, there are many examples of inspirational teaching of composition happening in schools, which must be celebrated. Students are inspired by teachers who are passionate about what they are teaching. I hope that through reading this book, you will find inspiration and useful tools to help encourage and motivate your own students in finding enjoyment in composing music.

How to use this book

Dip into this book whenever you want a flash of inspiration for your composing lessons: for classroom activity suggestions, different ways to approach composing in the classroom and practical advice for getting students engaged.

The ideas in this book are organised by theme – these are given at the foot of each page. Each idea follows a simple format:

○ **Title:** the catchy title sums up what the idea is about.

○ **Quote:** the opening quote from a student, teacher, composer or music educator captures the essence of the idea.

○ **Overview:** the quick overview of the idea will help you select a new idea or read or re-find an idea you found useful on a previous flick-through.

○ **Idea:** the idea itself.

○ **Hints and tips:** additional tips, suggestions for ways to take the idea further, handy hints and bonus ideas are provided throughout.

Visit **collins.co.uk/teachcomposition/download** for templates, tables, examples and suggested listening to accompany the ideas in this book.

A creative classroom 1

"Creativity is contagious; pass it on." (Albert Einstein)

How can we design a classroom environment that encourages our students to be imaginative, to develop their musical identity and to know that their creativity matters? Here are some practical suggestions for maximising the physical teaching area and building a positive culture.

The space

Ideally, an area conducive to musical creativity is well-resourced with instruments, recording equipment and computers. Teaching accommodation is often beyond our control, however, if possible, ensure there is enough physical space for students with 'breakout' areas too for individual and small group practical work.

○ Keep it versatile: Set up the classroom to enable a variety of musical activities.

○ Keep the classroom tidy: Take time to establish routines for handing out and collecting in equipment and always ensure that the classroom is ready for the next group.

Classroom culture

Establish a culture of acceptance. Students need to know that their endeavours will not be ridiculed or dismissed. (A set of classroom rules helps everyone stay on track and understand the boundaries.)

○ Always be positive.

○ Keep it musical: Provide opportunities in every lesson for students to listen to, play or create music.

○ Take risks: Students will feel more able to move out of their comfort zones if they see their teacher doing the same.

○ Lead by example: Students find it inspiring to see their teacher improvising and composing – aim to demonstrate creativity whenever possible.

Bonus idea

A 'Sharing board', presenting students' musical ideas, is a great way of displaying creativity and capturing ideas. To encourage dialogue, students could comment on each other's contributions.

Handy hint

To celebrate effort and achievement, start a 'Musician of the month' photo wall to highlight student triumphs. A certificate could be given out in assembly and a small prize awarded.

2 Compose from Day 1

"Let's see what these students can already do."

If we want to instil in our students a love of composing at GCSE, A-level and beyond, we must provide opportunities for them to develop these skills lower down the school. Here are some suggestions for making it a natural part of a music lesson rather than an occasional activity.

Initial composing task

Many teachers ask new students to complete a baseline test and fill in a questionnaire about their previous musical experiences. Include a short composing task at this point to aid subsequent lesson planning and give a general idea of student confidence levels, for example:

◖ Give students three notes, displayed clearly on a keyboard diagram. Ask them to create a short musical idea using the given pitches. Provide some prompts covering the basic musical elements (referred to as 'inter-related dimensions' in the KS3 National Curriculum).

◖ Write a list of contrasting moods on the board. Ask students to compose music in small groups to portray one of the moods. They then perform it to the class, who guess the mood.

◖ Give out some musical 'rule' cards (see Idea 8). Ask students to work in pairs to compose a short piece using the rules on their card.

Listening to inspire composition

Establish a listening routine, whether it is a listening journal (see Idea 4), regular starter activity or introducing a 'Composer of the week' series (see Idea 5). This is a sure way to be playing a wide variety of musical styles and inspiring composing activities.

Short composing tasks

Incorporating smaller composing tasks into music lessons ensures that students are regularly creating music and building confidence. An 'integrated approach' (see Idea 41) is an effective way to achieve this. Some classes may require a good deal of 'scaffolding' (see Idea 47) when they first start composing.

Bonus idea

Set up a composition portfolio for each student that remains with them throughout their time in school. It could be a virtual or physical folder of recordings, graphic scores, musical ideas and screenshots.

Ideas page

"Having somewhere I can write down all my ideas means that I don't have to worry if I forget something."

Encouraging students to use an *Ideas page* places value on the process of composing and not just on the final product. It provides space for students to capture musical ideas freely and the opportunity to revisit motifs not chosen for other activities.

If students are working solely on one composition in one place (e.g. at the computer), there can be a reluctance to try out and play around with different ideas for fear of 'messing up' the composition. One effective idea is to ask students to create an *Ideas page*:

○ The *Ideas page* can be a manuscript paper booklet, notation program or DAW file.

○ Students create a new file for each project where they can record/notate any motifs, themes or chord patterns that might be useful.

○ Student or teacher can add a sticky note/ text box to link it to the listening journal through referencing pieces that could provide inspiration and ideas, to encourage the connection between composing and listening activities.

○ Ask students to label and date each idea as a way to track their progress.

○ Once happy with an idea, students can transfer it over to their 'work-in-progress' composition file and develop it further.

○ To help students get the most out of using an *Ideas page*, create an example one or use another student's page to show them the layout and possible techniques to explore.

Using an *Ideas page* can make the whole process more enjoyable and encourages students to be creative and to explore different techniques.

Top tip

When used to its full potential, an *Ideas page* can be used as evidence for composing work – take it along to parents' evening and show it at school monitoring meetings.

Taking it further...

Set up a classroom 'Composing ideas board'. Students (and yourself) can pin up snippets of music they have come up with. If there is initial reluctance, share some of your own musical ideas or those of existing composers.

4 Listening journal

"Perceptive listening is the key to better musical understanding as well as more informed music composition skills." (Maud Hickey)

Whatever stage your students are at, a listening journal can be a valuable tool. Establishing this from the outset can pay dividends as students move up through the school, so that by GCSE and A-level, they have ingrained intentional listening as a habit and feel more confident using technical vocabulary.

Create a simple document that works for you and your students. Think carefully about the purpose of the listening journal and how you're going to use it (homework, starter activity, general classroom use, etc.). You might choose the listening material for students yourself, ask them to select their own pieces or a combination of the two.

- Follow up the listening journal and encourage class discussion at the start of each lesson.
- As new key words are introduced, encourage students to use these in their journals.
- Incorporate some friendly competition, e.g. give a prize each term to the class which has shown the most engagement and a 'Music critic of the year' to a student who has shown exceptional commitment.
- Students love to know what you're listening to – put a 'This week I am listening to…' sign on your door.
- Promote diversity by choosing some pieces by under-represented groups (see Handy hint).
- Variety keeps students engaged; throw in some quirky examples such as John Cage's *4'33"* and *She Who* by Jessica Curry, to stimulate discussion.
- Adopt the listening journal as a department focus – this will give value and consistency to the initiative, and benefit the whole music curriculum.

There are three sample templates online.

Handy hint

Promote diversity through your choices of listening. The following websites offer helpful databases and collections:
composerdiversity.com
musicbyblackcomposers.org
drakemusic.org

Composer of the week **5**

"My whole school gets involved with 'Composer of the week'."

Running a 'Composer of the week' series is a dynamic solution to the challenge of exposing students to a wide variety of styles, genres and artists to inspire their own composing. This initiative can get staff and students engaged, and provide a musical focus for the whole school.

Choose a range of composers representing different periods, nationalities and styles, and create a playlist for each composer on your preferred music platform. Choose six to ten pieces for each composer.

Set up a 'Composer of the week' display board and assign a small group of reliable students to update it. Promote it through your department's social media channels.

Music lessons

● If your students use a listening journal, encourage them to choose pieces by the composer of the week.

● Look for opportunities to link the composer of the week with your classroom activities or, if possible, build this more formally into the curriculum.

● As a starter activity, ask students to listen to a 'composer of the week' piece and answer questions or discuss with a partner.

Whole-school initiative

Get as many staff involved as possible. Send colleagues a weekly email with details of the next composer and suggested pieces, and make it easy for staff to access the music by creating a school music-streaming platform account. Ask staff for their favourite composers and include a profile on the 'Composer of the week' display board.

Play the music during the school day at some of these times or places: assembly, school reception, cafeteria, breakfast/after-school club, lesson changeover, P.E. changing rooms, tutor rooms…

Bonus idea

At the end of the school year, get everyone to vote for their favourite composer!

Top tip

If you haven't got time to create your own materials and playlists, BBC Radio 3 has a *Composer of the week* programme with useful supporting online resources such as a Composer A–Z and interviews with composers. (Search at **bbc.co.uk/ programmes**)

6 Active listening games

"The act of listening is in fact an act of composing." (John Cage)

Listening to music should be an enjoyable activity if we are to engage our students and get them enthused about different musical styles and genres. These simple ideas encourage active listening and can easily be adapted for different year groups and student ability levels.

Listening washing line (GCSE or A-level)

Fix a length of string from one corner of the classroom to the other. Hand out key word cards (about six per student/pair) and pegs (making sure they don't have the same words). Choose words such as: polyphonic, choral, glissando, pizzicato, sequence and improvisation.

Play a musical example that clearly demonstrates some of the key words. Invite students to peg up key words that apply to the music on the washing line. See if everyone agrees with the 'washing' words and discuss reasons.

Musical bingo

Give out one bingo card per student or group, and counters if using. Play a music excerpt (choose something that clearly demonstrates particular instruments, textures or devices). Students cross off an image/key word (could include instruments, dynamics, style/genre terms etc.), or place a counter on the appropriate space. Students shout, "Line!" and "Bingo!" when they have completed a line/whole grid.

> **Handy hint**
>
> Make your own bingo cards at: **toolsforeducators. com/bingo**

> **Taking it further...**
>
> Take one feature of the music you've been listening to, highlight the key word and create a practical task (e.g. at keyboards) around that key word.

Fill the board!

Divide the classroom whiteboard into two sections; one for each audio extract. Play each extract in turn. Whilst it is playing, invite two students at a time to come up to the front and each write down one word to describe the music. (Ask all students to write down their own ideas as well to ensure everyone is engaged.)

Afterwards, compare both sides of the board and identify any similarities. Invite students to come to the front to circle any words which are the same.

Composing club 7

"How are you catering for the 'musically curious' students in your school?"

Most music departments offer various extra-curricular ensembles for instrumentalists and singers, but for those students who have an interest in exploring sounds and playing about with musical ideas (AKA the 'musically curious'!) a 'Composing club' could fire their imaginations and take their skills to the next level.

Establishing a new club can be a challenge, especially if students already have a wide choice of clubs to attend. Identify the 'musically curious' students who may be interested in exploring composing outside of the classroom. Establish a 'core group' of loyal students to begin with – they will be your cheerleaders for the club and encourage others to attend.

Planning is key

In order to keep students motivated and engaged there needs to be a clear focus and plan for each session. If you are well-organised, students will see that you're taking the club seriously, and they will too.

Setting regular 'real-world' composing projects (see Idea 42) gives relevance and purpose to the composing activities. Make sure that there's an end point, to avoid a task dragging on aimlessly.

Motivation and attendance

If students are giving their time to attend, there must be a clear benefit to them. Offering something different to their usual classroom experience, such as the chance to try a different software program or use of the recording studio, can be a great incentive.

Establishing a simple routine for the session provides a sense of structure and value to the group. Meeting altogether at the start to discuss the aims of the session and answer any questions keeps everyone focused.

> **Top tip**
>
> Set up a dedicated online area for club members. Each week post a couple of listening suggestions, web links and musical ideas. This way if a student is away or you get held up, everyone has something to get on with.

> **Handy hint**
>
> Invite form tutors and heads of year to a sharing session at the end of each composing project to showcase students' work.

8 Stick to the rules

"I just can't think of anything to write!"

We've all had students who struggle to get started with a composing task and can't think of anything to write. Writing down some arbitrary 'rules' can remove some of the decisions that need to be made and give students a point of focus. This idea is a fun way to get some musical ideas going quickly.

Prepare some cards with three melody 'rules' written on, e.g. the examples below. Laminating them will make the cards last longer.

Demonstrate the activity at the front of the class first with your own rule card, creating a couple of short musical ideas.

Hand out the cards and give students five minutes to create a melody using the rules on the card.

Students play their musical ideas to the class and share the rules of their assigned card.

Extension task: ask students to write out their own set of rules based on key words that have been covered recently.

Top tip

This idea can easily be differentiated by writing out rules specifically for each student, giving more challenging rules to more confident students.

Your melody must:

- Include an octave leap
- Use some repeated notes
- Be in 6/8 time

Your melody must:

- Only use the notes of the blues scale
- Include triplets
- Move through two octaves

Musical consequences 9

"This idea is great as students don't have to write every part of the whole composition."

This idea for collaborative composing is based on the game 'Consequences', where a piece of paper is passed around a group with individuals contributing elements of the story and folding the paper over so the full story is only revealed at the end.

Two approaches can be taken:

1. Using a DAW

Each student creates a chord sequence on track 1, recording in time to the metronome.

Everyone moves round to the next computer, listens to what the previous student recorded and adds a drum beat.

Students move round again and add a riff.

Everyone moves again and adds some melodic material.

Finally, students return to their own computer and listen to what has been added to their original chord sequence.

2. Using a notation program

Set up a new score with four instruments (it is best to prescribe these or preload a template).

Each student inputs a four-bar melody line.

Everyone moves round to the next computer and adds a single-note bassline or chords to the melody line.

Students move round again and add a counter-melody.

Everyone moves again and adds one more musical feature.

> **Taking it further...**
>
> Students can use this activity to stimulate an individual composition in a similar style as it demonstrates the different layers of a composition and models the process of structuring and creating a simple piece.

10 Morse code rhythms

"I loved using the Morse code to create our own rhythms, it was so much fun!"

This idea is a fun way to get started with rhythm work. With some historical context added in, students can enjoy learning about the origin of Morse code and then using it to generate some fairly complex rhythms.

Composer, Barrington Pheloung, wrote the music for the television murder-mystery drama, *Inspector Morse*, which opens with a motif based on the Morse code for M-O-R-S-E. He was also known to hide rhythmic Morse code clues in the music, sometimes revealing the identity of the killer.

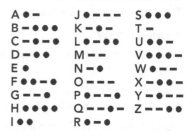

Demonstrate to the whole class how to spell out word rhythms using Morse code: use a crotchet for 'dash' and a quaver for 'dot'. Use student names or types of food, e.g. B-R-E-A-D would be:

Get everyone to clap the rhythms back, and ask students to help write the word, Morse code and corresponding rhythms on the board to show how it is worked out.

In pairs, ask students to choose a word to spell out as a rhythm. It can be helpful to assign one student as the pulse-keeper. Students clap their rhythms and share with the class.

Next, put two pairs of students together and ask them to teach each other their rhythms.

Extend the task by asking students to create a short musical performance of their group's rhythms using percussion instruments.

This activity can highlight a number of challenges, particularly concerning the notation of the rhythm, e.g. some words may require tied notes across the barline or create off-beat rhythms. Demonstrate first and ask students to have a go at notating their rhythms in pairs.

Moody intervals

"I never realised that great melodies had particular intervals that make us feel a certain way — it's powerful!"

Melodic intervals can stimulate a range of emotions and are useful in melody-writing when a composer wants to evoke a particular mood. This is a GCSE or A-level starter idea all about listening to melodies that successfully use intervals for effect.

You will need a variety of melodies that contain particular melodic intervals to evoke a specific mood (see suggestions below and online).

Play the examples, asking students to identify the overall mood of the melody/piece.

Then look more closely at the written melody and analyse the melodic intervals used.

Give students two contrasting moods and their corresponding melodic intervals and ask them to create two musical ideas to evoke these moods.

Taking it further...

After composing a melodic idea, students can explore harmony in a similar way, creating chords using the same interval.

Interval	Mood	Musical example	
		Piece	**Composer**
Minor second	Tense/ nervous	*Symphony no.9, 4th movement*	Antonín Dvořák
Augmented fourth (tritone)	Tense/ unsettled	*Maria* from *West Side Story*	Leonard Bernstein
Perfect fourth	Neutral/ peaceful	*Notturno* from *A Midsummer Night's Dream*	Felix Mendelssohn
Perfect fifth	Triumphant/ brave/ optimistic	*Flying Theme* from *E.T.*	John Williams
Perfect octave	Positive/ brave/ optimistic	*Somewhere over the Rainbow* from *The Wizard of Oz*	Harold Arlen

12 Composition speed dating

"I love going round the room listening to and commenting on my friends' work"

Peer-assessing composition is a great way for students to share ideas and give helpful feedback. Use this fun idea when students are working on individual compositions at computers. After using it in one lesson as a plenary, it can then form the starter task for the next lesson – students use the sheet to set targets for the lesson.

Taking it further...

Peer-assess in this way once every half-term. Students will enjoy tracking each others' progress and feeling that their advice is helpful as well as getting ideas for their own composition.

Bonus idea !

Instead of using paper, have a document open on the computer for students to type in their comments and save, to retrieve easily in the next lesson.

○ Give a blank speed dating sheet to each student (see below). This stays at the computer workstation.

○ 15–20 minutes before the end of the lesson, students save their work, leave their computers and move to the next workstation.

○ Using headphones, students listen to their classmate's composition and write down on the sheet two positive comments and one suggestion for their 'to do' list next lesson.

○ Everyone then moves in the same direction to the next computer. Repeat a few times, so that there are at least three sets of comments written down. (To make it even more fun, why not time the class for two minutes per 'date' and sound a bell when it is time to move on!)

○ Leave five minutes at the end for them to return to their computer and read their sheet.

'Date' name	Two positive points	One point for the 'to do' list	Other comments

Wrong melody

"It's easier to say what's wrong with a tune than what's right with it!"

In this idea, students take on the role of 'teacher' and highlight the limitations and positive points with some given melodies. It is a versatile activity that can be used as a starter or plenary.

Create some examples in your preferred notation software of melodies that deliberately don't 'work', e.g. the key is very unclear; the melody doesn't flow and contains lots of rests; there is disjunct movement; it has a very narrow range and is stuck around a few notes.

Demonstrate this activity first at the front of the class with one example 'wrong melody'. Display it on the whiteboard and play it for students. Ask for observations as to why the melody is not successful.

Give students the prepared 'wrong' melodies to mark, asking them to provide detailed feedback on the weaknesses that they find. Students can complete this exercise individually, in pairs or as a whole class, in several ways:

❍ At the computer, using notation software.

❍ On paper, playing the melodies at a keyboard.

❍ As a whole-class activity with the melodies displayed on the whiteboard.

After marking the melodies, ask students to offer ideas for improvement and rewrite the melody.

Top tip

Tips for good melody-writing:
Establishes a clear sense of key.
Has a sense of direction.
Demonstrates a good melodic shape.
Has some kind of 'defining feature' (see Idea 33).
Shows a clear sense of phrasing.

14 Cryptograms

"We looked at how Shostakovich used his initials to create a theme, so I did the same in my composition!"

A cryptogram is a sequence of notes where there is a relationship between the note names and letters. Introducing students to cryptography can provide a fun starting point for creating an initial motif.

Composers such as J.S. Bach, Johannes Brahms and Dimitri Shostakovich all used cryptograms in their compositions – it was a way of adding their signature to the music or paying homage to a fellow composer. For example, Shostakovich used the DSCH motif in many of his compositions, including *Symphony no.15* and *String Quartet no.8 in C minor*, and J.S. Bach used the 'B-A-C-H' motif in the final movement of *Art of Fugue*.

Taking it further...

Once students have their motif, use it to explore different development techniques. They could create an 'Ideas page' (see Idea 3) and try varying the rhythm, extending the melody, adding a counter-melody and adding chords.

Bonus idea

Create a class composition in a workshop-style lesson using everyone's name motifs. This could be a rondo form piece with your own name as the alternating 'A' section.

D-S-C-H motif

B-A-C-H motif

Most names/initials don't correspond directly with pitch names – unsurprising, given that there are only seven pitches to choose from – but don't let that put you off. Solfa Cipher is a website which turns code into melodies: **wmich.edu/mus-theo/solfa-cipher/**. You can type in any name, and a musical code is generated. You can see the notated code, listen to it and download the MIDI file. Why not get students to either create their own musical code from scratch or type their names into Solfa Cipher and use the motif produced? This can be a good starting point for teaching compositional techniques (see Ideas 32–9) as the original theme or motif is already written.

Don't reinvent the wheel 15

"Lesser artists borrow, great artists steal." (Igor Stravinsky)

Composers down the centuries have borrowed from each other, transformed ideas and made them their own. This idea is about showing students that you don't always have to come up with something completely original; it is OK to reuse a chord sequence or melodic fragment...

Listen to some examples to demonstrate how composers have borrowed from each other, e.g.

● Compare *Trio Sonata in G major* by Domenico Gallo and *Overture to Pulcinella* by Stravinsky.

● *Scherzo* from *Symphony no.5* by Beethoven borrows from the *Finale* of *Symphony no.40* by Mozart.

● Richard Strauss borrowed themes from Bruch's Violin Concerto no.1 (2nd movement) in *An Alpine Symphony*.

● Compare *Mass in A minor* by Imogen Holst with *Mass in G minor* by Ralph Vaughan Williams.

Re-use an existing chord pattern

Give students a chord sequence from an existing piece and ask them to compose their own melody over the top. For a simple starting point, ask students to play the chords from *Canon in D* by Johann Pachelbel. Get one student to improvise a melody whilst the other provides the harmony.

Re-use a short melodic extract

Give students a choice of melodic extracts from an unfamiliar piece or compose a couple of bars yourself. Ask them to continue the melody to create a 16-bar section. It is a good idea to demonstrate this activity first.

> **Taking it further...**
>
> Provide prompts to help students extend their ideas, e.g.
> How can you use the existing rhythmic cells and melodic intervals?
> Can the underpinning harmony be altered?
> Will it work in a different key or time signature?
> What will it sound like in a different register?

Example extract:

16 Rhythm grid

"A simple rhythm grid is a clear and versatile tool to get students creating music and performing as a group."

The beauty of the rhythm grid is that it is really easy to adapt 'on the spot' in lessons and can be differentiated to cater for every student. It's an effective starter activity that can easily spill over into the main class activity and get students confident about feeling the pulse and reading simple rhythms.

○ Draw out a grid and key on the whiteboard (you can add more players once the activity is established), for example:

	1	2	3	4	5	6	7	8
Player 1	✓	✓	✓		✓	✓	✓	
Player 2		★		★		★		★
Player 3			♥	♥			♥	♥
Player 4	✗		✗		✗			✗

Key:
✓ = hand clap   ★ = foot stamp   ♥ = palm slide   ✗ = finger click

○ Explain how the grid works and demonstrate each body percussion action.

○ Ask students to perform each line as a class, with you tapping out an eight-beat pulse, before combining different lines. You may need to count the beats out loud to begin with.

○ Once you are happy that students can perform each pattern, start to put them together. Aim to stop calling out the beats once you feel that students are confident using the grid.

Extend the activity by: adding more rhythmic lines and more complex rhythmic cells, e.g. introduce triplets (three symbols in one box); adding pitch; moving students to work in small groups to create their own grid using body percussion or percussion instruments.

> **Top tip**
>
> Once students are using the rhythm grid, show how their composition would look using staff notation. Encourage students to begin notating their rhythms, if appropriate.

Throw a dice! 17

"I never knew that Mozart played dice games to create music!"

This idea draws on a method used by Charles Ives and John Cage (amongst others), and explores the use of random musical elements. This is known as 'aleatoric music' – music by chance. It's a fun and exciting way to compose, as no performance will ever be the same twice, and it can serve as a good starting point for creating music.

For this idea, you will either need lots of dice or to create your own using a template (search 'dice template' online): Two sets of dice will be needed per pupil pair – one for pitch and one for rhythm. Model the activity with the whole class first.

Dice 1: Pitch generator – choose six notes to represent each number, e.g. 1 = A, 2 = E, 3 = F♯ etc.

Dice 2: Rhythm generator – choose six note values to represent each number (it works best if one or two are used more than once), e.g. 1 = minim, 2 = two quavers, 3 = crotchet, 4 = crotchet etc.

Choose a time signature and agree on a time limit or number of throws for the activity. Students take it in turns to roll the dice to generate each beat of the composition. For example, Student 1 (pitch dice) might throw a 'D' and Student 2 (rhythm dice) might throw a minim.

Students add each beat to their composition, notating it on manuscript paper. They can decide which octave the pitches are written in. If students struggle with this, they can write out the rhythm sequence with each pitch labelled above as letters.

Once the time limit is reached, students attempt to play the composition. Encourage discussion about the process and musical outcome.

Mozart's dice game

Composers in the 18th century loved playing musical dice games, known as 'Die Musikalisches Wufelspiel'. Mozart is said to have written music in this way – try it yourself online: **playonlinedicegames.com/mozart**

Taking it further...

To extend this activity, try adding rests, changing time signatures or adding more dice, representing other musical elements, such as tempo and dynamics (add six tempo markings or dynamic markings to each dice).

Teaching tip

See suggested listening examples online.

18 Improvising

"The 'no such thing as a mistake' concept opens up an environment where creativity is never stifled." (Walter Thompson)

Improvisation is spontaneous composition and students should have plenty of opportunity to explore their creativity in this way. Many of us encourage students to improvise as part of a KS3 blues topic; this is an idea for facilitating group improvisation and composition in real-time.

Soundpainting is another form of aleatoric music (see Idea 17) and it can be a useful pre-cursor to, or break from, more structured improvisation and composition activities. Created by American composer, Walter Thompson, it is a live composing sign language with more than 1,500 gestures that are signed by the Soundpainter (composer) to express the type of material desired of the performers.

Stand in front of the group and have students seated with instruments and/or voices ready. It doesn't matter which notes they choose to play/sing: you, the Soundpainter, compose in real time with whatever sounds happen, and students have the opportunity to improvise, perform and explore sound.

Taking it further...

For something a bit different in a school concert, why not perform a live composing session using Soundpainting?

Handy hint

There are plenty of resources including workbooks and videos, available at **soundpainting.com**

Start by learning a handful of gestures and aim to build up your repertoire (watch a workshop video of the method in action – see Handy hint).

Introduce each sign to the group one at a time, speak as little as possible and get students to follow your signals. You could even challenge yourself to do a whole lesson without saying a word!

Once students are familiar with the signs, choose someone else to be the Soundpainter and direct the group.

One-pitch composition **19**

"You can do so much with just one note!"

Starting with a one-note composition may sound a bit simple and unexciting. However, through removing elements such as melody, harmony and tonality, space is created for students to focus on other aspects of the composition, like rhythm and structure.

This idea can be adapted and developed for use with KS3 and GCSE classes as a compositional starting point and can easily be extended into a larger-scale project.

Play Ligeti's *Musica Ricercata* (see online resources for alternative listening suggestions), and ask students to discuss how the composer has created a whole piece based on just one note.

Choose a note and demonstrate on an instrument how different elements, such as tempo, register, rhythm, dynamics and structure, can be applied to create a short composition. (This could be composed in advance.)

Ask students to use instruments to write their own one-note piece. It can be helpful to provide some prompts (see below) – these could be presented as musical rule cards (see Idea 8).

One-note composition task prompts

❍ How can you use rhythm to create a sense of excitement?

❍ What effect does changing the time signature have?

❍ Can you include different instrumental techniques?

❍ Can you include a short motif that can be repeated and aid the structural organisation?

❍ How does your composition start and finish?

❍ Are you exploring the full range of your instrument?

> **Taking it further...**
>
> Ask students to compose a series of short one-note movements portraying different moods or colours, for a group of instruments.

20 Pitches and modes

"Different modes, different moods."

Scales and modes are an excellent starting point for creating music. Modes are particularly accessible as some use only the white notes on the keyboard. This idea for KS3 students explores using modes as a stimulus for composing a melody, adding a bass part and thinking about mood and atmosphere.

The list below summarises the seven modes and their characteristics. They have all been written on C for comparison (a detailed table including listening examples is included online).

Ionian: bright (major scale)

Dorian: dark

Phrygian: exotic and dark

Lydian: bright and mysterious

Mixolydian: bright, tinged with sadness

Aeolian: sad

Locrian: unsettling

Starter activity: Which number?

○ This fun game introduces modes and encourages a focussed atmosphere at the start of a lesson.

○ Play a C major scale (Ionian mode) on the piano at the front of the class, numbering each note out loud. Explain that in the next scale you play two notes will have changed and students are to identify the numbers of these notes.

○ Now play the Dorian mode whilst counting the numbers out loud and ask students to identify which number notes had changed (3 and 7). Do the same for each of the modes, returning to the original Ionian mode in between playings.

Classroom activity

○ Following the starter activity, listen to some examples of modes in existing pieces (see online resources). Discuss the mood and characteristics of the music.

○ Choose one mode to focus on and ask students to play it several times on the keyboard.

○ Demonstrate improvising on the given mode and then ask students to have a go. To extend the task ask students to play a left-hand drone of one or two notes (notes 1 and 5) of the mode whilst improvising with the right hand.

○ Thinking about the mood or characteristic of the chosen mode (sad, dark, bright, etc.), ask students to compose a melody using the notes from the mode, to reflect that mood.

○ Introduce the idea of 'tonic' as a 'home-note' to start and finish on, making the phrase sound complete.

○ Highlight other musical elements that could be brought into play, e.g. tempo, instrumentation, pitch, rhythm and phrasing.

○ Ask students to perform their melodies.

Extension: add a drone bass part using the tonic and one other note (usually dominant).

Bonus idea

Combine this idea with different starter activities (e.g. Ideas 8–13) and deeper exploration of melody-writing (Ideas 33–35).

Taking it further...

This activity could lead into a larger composing project. Students could write a song or instrumental piece, based on the mode. More confident students could explore harmony and accompaniment or compose a counter-melody (see Idea 36). You could also introduce world music scales such as Indian raga, Persian, Flamenco and Slendro/Pelog scales.

21 Rhythm

"There is music wherever there is rhythm, as there is life wherever there beats a pulse." (Igor Stravinsky)

Of all the musical elements, rhythm potentially has the scope to transform an average composition into a memorable masterpiece. Once you've got students playing in time to a steady beat, clapping different patterns and exploring rhythmic cells, they can begin to transfer these skills into their own composing activities.

First, get students doing a Mexican wave! Not only does this inject some energy into the lesson but it also demonstrates the concept of going round the circle one at a time and not starting until the adjacent person has played.

Bonus idea

The *How music works* series by Howard Goodall (available on YouTube) includes a fascinating episode on rhythm which is well worth watching with students.

Top tip

If students find it difficult to maintain rhythms individually, put them in pairs/small groups to clap a rhythm together, or get them to do the activity with their eyes closed!
For more class rhythm activities see Ideas 10 and 16.
Recommended listening is provided in the online resources.

○ All sit in a circle and use a metronome or keep a beat playing to keep everyone in time.

○ One student (or yourself) starts the 'rhythm machine' by clapping a simple rhythm and repeating it over and over as an ostinato.

○ The next student adds a rhythm over the first one and also repeats it as an ostinato, and this continues until the whole group is clapping a rhythm.

○ The 'rhythm machine' then goes into reverse mode, with the first student dropping out, then the second one and so on until there is only one student left clapping a rhythm.

This activity can be repeated using percussion instruments, then keyboards and orchestral instruments, if available. Invite a confident pulse-keeper to hold the group together and use non-verbal signals to support the ensemble. Encourage students to experiment with rests, off-beat rhythms and adding occasional extra beats to provide some unpredictability. It may work well to divide the class into smaller groups.

Harmony 22

"Tension and release..."

Musical dissonance is a powerful device in creating (and resolving) tension and has huge potential for various composing projects. This idea focuses on creating dissonance as a means of exploring harmony through composing in three short activities culminating in one larger composing task.

1. Suspended chords

Suspended chords are often found in film music. They simultaneously create an open and tense sound. The third of the chord is replaced with a second or fourth, both of which want to resolve to the third.

❍ Using sustained strings on a keyboard, DAW or notation program, ask students to create a short passage using suspended second or fourth chords.

2. Note clusters

Note clusters are chords consisting of at least three adjacent notes, though they can include any other notes too.

❍ Get students creating their own cluster chords with dissonant intervals: minor/major second, minor/major seventh, and augmented fourth (tritone). Ask students to add a rhythm to their chord and play over their suspended chord passage from Activity 1.

3. Diminished seventh chord

A diminished seventh chord is constructed through building a stack of four notes, each a minor third apart (root, minor third, diminished fifth, diminished seventh). It is perfect for adding colour or creating an unsettled atmosphere. To resolve the tension the chord resolves to a diatonic chord (often the dominant).

❍ Use boomwhackers or a giant keyboard mat to demonstrate how to build a diminished seventh chord. At keyboards (using sustained strings), assign each student a single note to be held, gradually building up the chord.

Student composing task

Give students an unsettling stimulus, e.g. a poem, image or character. Using the three devices above, students compose a short piece depicting the stimulus. You could provide some success criteria (see Idea 43) and use a radar diagram for assessment (Idea 48).

23 Texture

"I loved listening to how different string instruments could sound together."

To really grasp the potential of exploring texture in composition, students need to be listening to and playing a wide variety of music. This idea focuses on string texture, and works well with A-level classes. However, it can easily be adapted for younger students and a different instrumental family by changing the listening.

Play the *Main Theme* from *Psycho* by Bernard Herrman and ask students to describe the texture. Highlight the closeness of the string part-writing, register and playing technique.

Next, play Stravinsky's *Augers of Spring* from *The Rite of Spring* and note the similarities and differences.

As a group, clap the opening rhythm of the *Augers of Spring*, stamping on the accented beats. Extend this task by asking students to play the opening on their instruments or at keyboards, dividing the chord if necessary.

Learn the *Psycho* theme as a class or in pairs, dividing the chord if required. Invite students to experiment with pitch, rest placement and rhythm to explore the effects on mood.

Now play and follow in the score the opening passage from Sowande's *African Suite: II Nostalgia: Andante*. Discuss the string texture.

Ask students to consider all three pieces and discuss what the difference in mood and musical texture is and how it is achieved. (Other listening suggestions in online resources.)

Taking it further...

Ask students to find more examples of pieces with different string textures and add them to their listening journals (see Idea 4).

Composing task

Students write a short passage for strings (provide a chord pattern, if appropriate) in either a menacing or tranquil mood. They should think about: instrumental ranges, part-writing, rhythmic motifs and placement of rests. Use notation software or a DAW (it is important that students explore the string sounds and experiment with different textures).

Timbre and sonority 24

"Playing with timbre is like a painter mixing colours — it can transform the whole work."

Timbre is often described as 'the tone colour of an instrument'. Sonority is a similar term but tends to apply to a group of instruments or overall soundscape. Exploring the different sounds and capabilities of various instruments is exciting, especially if you have a range of real instruments available, but DAWs and notation programs can be used if not. This idea explores timbre through the sound source, playing techniques and combining sounds.

Sound source

Ask your visiting music teachers and/or students to demonstrate their instruments and discuss how the sounds are produced.

❍ Play examples of solo instruments (**audionetwork.com** has samples) and ask students to: identify the instrument/family; describe how the sound is produced; and choose one adjective to describe the timbre (dry, metallic, scratchy, etc.).

Playing technique

Most instruments are capable of producing a range of timbres. Explore different techniques, demonstrating where possible.

❍ Give students a selection of titles, e.g. 'The playful pixie', 'Moon on the water', 'Falling ice crystals'… Ask them to create a short passage using an instrument's timbre to represent the stimulus. Use a DAW or real instruments.

The combination of sounds

Play examples of orchestral sections playing together, e.g. Britten's *The Young Person's Guide to the Orchestra* and Perry's *A Short Piece for Orchestra*.

❍ Give students a simple passage of music (e.g. a keyboard piece they are learning) and ask them to arrange it for different groups of instruments, with a focus on techniques, using a keyboard, notation program or DAW.

> **Top tip**
>
> Don't forget the voice! Play examples by Ella Fitzgerald, Kate Bush and Kiri Te Kanawa (or other diverse singers) to demonstrate variations in voice timbre. Suggested wider listening is provided in the online resources.

25 Structure and form

"A composition must have a beginning, a middle and an end."

A composition needs structure. A strong beginning will capture the listener's attention, but what happens in the middle and how will it be concluded? This idea looks at three ways of exploring musical structure at KS3 or GCSE level, through composing in groups, pairs or as individuals.

Musical beginnings

A composition should have a convincing start – this doesn't necessarily mean it must be loud and dramatic.

❍ Share with students the opening lines from some novels (suggestions in online resources) and discuss their impact. Draw a parallel with music through playing examples of strong musical openings (suggestions in online resources). Ask students to compose a musical opening with impact, considering the various musical elements.

Repeating ideas: class rondo

Get a collaborative class rondo going with everyone composing a section of the piece!

❍ Give students an eight-bar melody (A) to learn on keyboards. Then ask students to compose their own eight-bar melody, either in the same key or a related key. (See Ideas 13, 33, 34 and 35 for further ideas on melody-writing.) Perform the rondo with everyone playing melody A, alternating with individual student melodies (B, C, D, etc.).

Telling a story

A fun way to get students structuring musical ideas is to write a short story in groups to be 'performed' with a narrator and music following the pattern: introduce two characters; dramatic event; conclusion.

❍ Compose a motif for each character. Make the event dramatic using dynamics, tempo and instrumentation. How can the ending be reflected in the music?

Bonus idea

Find out which set texts your students are studying in English and try to incorporate these into the activity.

Handy hint

When listening, play some examples that feature small ensembles or soloists and not just a full orchestra. Students can feel intimidated when they begin to compose if the only examples they have heard are for huge forces. It is even better if you perform some examples yourself!

Fanfare 26

"I loved writing a fanfare for our school prize-giving!"

Composing a fanfare is a great starter project for KS3 or GCSE students – it can be short in length, uses repetition, triadic movement and focuses on one instrumental family. Everyone can write something that fits the brief fairly easily and there's plenty of scope for more confident students to develop their musical skills further.

Before starting this composition task, introduce the genre by playing and listening to examples (see suggested preparation activities online).

Listen to some fanfare examples (suggestions online) and identify the types of rhythmic motifs used, e.g. dotted rhythms, use of anacrusis, quaver and two semiquavers, triplets, etc.

Play the **Pin number game:** write ten one-beat rhythmic cells on the board, numbered 0–9. Clap four-beat sequences and ask students to identify the pin number. Create a fanfare bank of one- and two-bar motifs (examples online). Students may create their own motifs or choose two from the bank. Encourage them to use punchy repeated notes, crisp dotted rhythms and triadic figures.

Demonstrate how to combine and develop the motifs to create a memorable fanfare tune.

Support students to add tonic and dominant block chords to accompany their melody (see Idea 38 for further tips on adding chords to a melody).

Extension: Encourage students to: use melodic decoration, include inversion chords, experiment with texture, compose a contrasting section in a new key.

Top tip

Writing a fanfare is the perfect opportunity to explore the brass and percussion families. If possible get your VMTs (Visiting Music Teachers) involved and any brass/percussion players in the class.

Taking it further...

The Royal Opera House runs an annual fanfare competition for young people. They provide online resources and materials: **roh.org.uk/learning/young-people/fanfare/resources**. Why not run your own fanfare competition in school? The winning entry could be performed at the school prize-giving.

27 Waltz

"The characteristic oom-pah-pah accompaniment makes chord-writing more accessible."

A waltz doesn't necessarily have to be in the traditional Viennese style – with some exploration we can find a number of waltzes in different styles that can spark students' imaginations and get them composing. This idea outlines example steps for composing a waltz for GCSE students.

◉ Suggested listening: The following pieces are great examples to introduce the concept: *Waltz* from *The Sleeping Beauty* by Pytor Illyich Tchaikovsky; *The Blue Danube* by Johann Strauss Jr.; *The Birthday Party Waltz* by Horace Weston; *Divertimento: II Waltz* by Leonard Bernstein; *Scarf Dance* by Cécile Chaminade.

◉ Instrumentation: It is a good idea to guide students in their selection of instruments. They could start with a melody instrument and piano accompaniment, and add other parts in later, if necessary.

◉ Compose a melody: Support students to compose an eight-bar waltz melody using mainly stepwise movement. It should clearly establish the key and be rhythmically straightforward. (See Ideas 33–5 for more help with melody-writing.)

Extension: More advanced students may wish to compose a counter-melody (see Idea 36) to develop the initial theme.

◉ Add an accompaniment: Chords will mostly be I, IV and V. Encourage students to adopt the characteristic 'oom-pah-pah' accompaniment style, highlighting the root notes of each chord on 'oom'. (See Idea 38 for support with adding chords to a melody.)

◉ Structure: A ternary form structure (ABA) works well, but there is obviously scope for more advanced students to develop this or try something different. A key change to the relative major/minor or dominant offers contrast in the middle.

Taking it further...

Ask students to arrange their waltz for an ensemble at school, e.g. orchestra, string group or mixed ensemble.

"This topic is always a winner!"

Film music is a really popular topic at KS3 and KS4, with engaging listening material, clever musical 'tricks' and the opportunity to compose directly to a film clip using computer software. This idea provides a number of short composing tasks. Students can combine the skills learnt from these tasks to compose music for a longer film/video game clip.

○ **Compose a leitmotif:** Use different scales/modes (see Idea 20 for modes) to compose character leitmotifs, e.g. major scale for the hero; minor scale for the villain; whole-tone scale for a good magical character; chromatic scale for an evil magical character.

○ **Develop the leitmotif:** Ideas could include: adding a contrasting counter-melody (see Idea 36); changing the time signature; writing it in the relative minor/major; exploring different rhythmic possibilities.

○ **Try 'Mickey-mousing':** This technique synchronises the action exactly with the music and is often used in comedy scores. Import a short animated film clip, e.g. *Wallace and Gromit* or *Angry Birds*, for students to compose music to.

○ **Set the scene:** Give students an image or written description of a scene to plan and write music for, e.g. tropical beach; cemetery at night; bustling city; fairground; stormy sea. Challenge more able students by adding an unexpected element to the scene, e.g. a stranded mermaid; lost child in the city; Komodo dragon in the forest.

Explore different film genres

Compile a portfolio of film genres and their musical features for quick reference in short composing tasks (see online resources).

Handy hint

If you don't have access to computers, get students in groups using body percussion and instruments to create suspense through exploring the musical elements.

Bonus idea

Introduce this topic by watching *The Power of Music in Film: How music affects film:* **youtu. be/iSkJFs7myn0**

---

29 Theme and variations

"I didn't realise that so much could be done with Twinkle, Twinkle Little Star!"

Theme and variations is a brilliant way to teach the elements of music through composition. Everything can be covered in an accessible way through exploring melody, harmony, rhythm, texture, instrumentation, dynamics and tempo.

Listen to examples of theme and variations, e.g. *Ah! Vous dirai-je, Maman* by Mozart (other examples are listed online). Use a simple grid to help students to organise their thoughts whilst listening – this will kick start the planning process and give plenty of options for students as they start to compose.

Ah! Vous dirai-je, Maman by Mozart					
	Theme	**Variation 1**	**Variation 2**	**Variation 3**	**Variation 4**
Character/mood					
Key					
Melody					
Harmony					
Rhythm					

Composing a theme and variations

○ Instrumentation: Students may wish to write for their own instrument, within an ensemble, or for solo piano. Composing for a group will give more scope for variation and provide a challenge for more able students.

○ Compose the theme melody: The challenge here is to keep it simple! Many students make the original tune over-complicated, making it harder to develop later on. It's worth spending time getting the theme right. Alternatively, choose an existing melody.

Once the theme is chosen or composed, show students how to transpose it into the relative major or minor, ready for one of the variations.

○ Write four or five variations: The further we get from the original theme, the more different the variations become. Some ideas for variations include the following (adapt for the age and experience of your students):

○ Melody – adding passing notes; arpeggiating the melody; changing the octave; ornamentation; including melodic sequence; augmenting or diminishing intervals.

○ Harmony and tonality – if students have composed their own theme, they will first need to add chords. Explore substitute chords for later variations; use a pedal note; add some suspensions; modulate within a variation.

○ Rhythm – adding an anacrusis; putting a rest on the first beat of the bar; introducing triplets; adding dotted rhythms; creating cross-rhythms with the accompaniment.

○ Texture – melody and accompaniment; imitative movement between parts; two-part texture; add octaves; homophonic texture. Different textures can be explored within a single variation, e.g. it could start with the theme in octaves, moving into a homophonic passage where the theme is harmonised.

Bonus idea !

Variations on an Elizabethan Theme (1953) is a quirky piece whereby several composers (including Britten, Walton, Tippett and Berkley) each contributed a variation on *Sellinger's Round* for string orchestra. Try this as a class project. Provide a theme and each student composes a variation!

30 Minimalism

"Less is more."

Minimalist music is a popular topic at KS3 and also features as an area of study on some exam board specifications. The clear compositional techniques used in this style make it a good option for a composition project or technical study.

Although minimalism appears to be simple because of the repetitive style and seemingly straightforward techniques, it is far from easy to compose in this style. Below are some ideas for getting students composing with a 'less is more' attitude. It can work well to create a series of shorter technical 'studies' in a portfolio if a full composition doesn't suit your students/timeframe/resources.

○ **Compose a motif:** Create a simple one-bar motif using (possibly using the pentatonic scale). This will be the basis of the composition. The rhythm should be simple and could include some rests, for example:

○ **Record the motif:** If using a DAW, ask students to record it on a single track four times. It is a good idea to have the metronome on and to play it at a slower tempo when recording.

○ **Add a bass line:** A descending stepwise bass line can work well with a repetitive melody line (see example online).

○ **Extend the motif:** Start by asking students to use note addition by adding one more note progressively to extend the melody:

Later on in the piece, note subtraction can be used, where each note is gradually taken away.

Other ideas for developing the motif (see online resources)

○ **Rhythmic augmentation/diminution:** To lengthen or shorten the original idea. This is an effective way to reinforce learning on note values.

○ Layering: Encourage students to explore creating a layered texture incorporating the techniques above. Minimalist music characteristically starts with a single line with instruments being added gradually to reach a climactic point. This can make compositions rather lengthy, though students can try this technique on a smaller scale.

○ Phase shifting: Start the same motif in two different parts. Change the rhythm slightly through shortening or lengthening the motif in one part. The two parts will now go in and out of sync.

Taking it further...

Once students have explored using different minimalist techniques, they can develop these ideas into a full composition, thinking about overall structure and the gradual building up of musical texture.

Handy hint

Challenge your students to perform Steve Reich's *Clapping Music* – there are plenty of YouTube videos to choose from and it could even feature in your next concert!

31 Song-writing

"Chords or melody first?"

When teaching song-writing we may need to try a few different approaches until we find one that works for our students. Some teachers swear by starting with a chord sequence whilst others insist that the best way is to start with the melody. Why not let the students decide...

Chords first

Give students a chord sequence: I – V – vi – IV has an optimistic feel, whereas vi – IV – I – V can be used for a more melancholy song. Alternatively ask students to create their own chord pattern.

Get students to hum or sing over the top of the chord pattern. Demonstrate this first and make a couple of 'deliberate' mistakes so that the class can see that it won't be perfect first time.

Top tip

Students need to have confidence in singing themselves if they are to write an effective song, so it's a good idea to get classes singing on a regular basis.

Taking it further...

If your school hosts a 'Battle of the bands' event, why not get students to write a song in pairs or small groups to be performed? See Idea 19 for further exploration of a one-note approach to composition.

If lyrics have already been chosen/written, students can use these to improvise further and begin to shape their ideas.

Keep it simple! Use peer appraisal tasks to get students reviewing their classmates' melodies and asking: could it be simpler?

Another approach is to use notes from the chord sequence and add passing notes to create stepwise melodic movement. This is not the most imaginative approach, but will be suitable for some students.

Melody first

Most melodies in popular songs are simple and punchy. Take a leaf out of Taylor Swift's book and try a one-note melody approach. Students can create a simple, short motif and vary the rhythm to reflect the natural shape of the lyrics.

The 'hook' – a good starting point for the chorus is to come up with a catchy hook. Limit the number of pitches students can use to avoid over-complication. Using the pentatonic scale usually yields good results.

Circle of fifths

"The circle of fifths is one of the most powerful musical devices!"

The circle of fifths is an important compositional tool that can be used to teach keys, chord progressions, writing bass lines, modulation and notation. This idea gives an example KS3 composition activity using it to generate chord sequences.

With some simple explanation, the circle of fifths can be taught in an engaging way that gives students a solid understanding of chords and keys, useful for their own composing activities. This activity uses the 'integrated approach' (see Idea 41). The following stages do not necessarily need to happen in this order.

● **Listen:** Choose two or three musical examples that clearly show the circle of fifths progression. (*Fly Me to the Moon* by Bart Howard is a great example. Other examples are listed in the online resources.)

● **Analyse:** Look at the bass line and chords of the chosen examples. Create an activity with an excerpt of a circle of fifths passage and some chords missing. Students use the circle of fifths diagram (see online resources) to fill in the missing chords.

● **Perform:** Give students differentiated parts of *Fly Me to the Moon* (or other suitable piece) and work towards a class performance.

Compose
● **Create a circle of fifths chord sequence:**
Use the circle of fifths diagram to write a chord pattern. It is easiest to start off with two chords per bar and then work on the rhythm in more detail later. Introduce added-note chords such as 7th chords, as an extension.

● **Write a strong bass line:** Show students how to pick out the root of each chord to create the bass line.

● **Compose a melody:** With the chords and bass line in place, students can now create the melody. It is helpful to go back and listen again to examples. Encourage simplicity.

> **Handy hint**
>
> Encourage the students to complete the above steps using instruments as much as possible so that they are playing and internalising the musical patterns.

33 Defining features

"The Defining Feature Approach® combines a creative starting point with a structured method."

A 'defining feature' in a melody is a musical idea that is repeated several times and gives the tune its overall character. This idea explores the use of defining features as a starting point for composing a great tune!

If you listen to and look closely at memorable melodies, you can start to identify their 'defining feature'. Defining features can be categorised in three ways: by interval, by rhythm or by contour.

By interval

Example: the use of the major third interval in Grieg's, *In the Hall of the Mountain King*, particularly the descending major third sequence which creates tension and gives the melody its sense of unease:

Key:
● Chromatic movement ○ Major thirds

By rhythm

Many great themes include a defining rhythmic feature such as a triplet, dotted rhythm, off-beat or anacrusis. Examples include: *Dance of the Knights (Montagues and Capulets)* from *Romeo and Juliet* by Sergei Prokofiev, *Eliza's Aria* by Elena Kats-Chernin and *James Bond Theme* by John Barry.

By contour

Melodies defined by contour tend to be: longer (e.g. eight bars), rhythmically simple, include considered use of the rise and fall of pitch and use melodic intervals intentionally. Examples include: *Main Title* from *Chocolat* by Rachel Portman and *Londonderry Air*. Using contour as a defining feature can work well with advanced students composing a more substantial theme.

Using defining features as a compositional starting point

O Demonstrate some examples: Play a couple of catchy tunes to the students with the melodies displayed on the whiteboard (suggestions in online resources). Explore what the character of the melody is and try to identify the 'defining feature'.

O Explore the defining feature: Give students the defining feature you've been exploring, e.g. a major third or a triplet rhythm. Ask them to play/clap it back.

O Use the defining feature: Ask students to create their own musical idea based on that defining feature. Leave the task quite open-ended with the only parameter being that the defining feature must be obvious and repeated. (See Idea 34 for ways to help students to refine and extend their 'defining feature' motif into a satisfying melodic theme.)

Handy hint

Visit **icancompose.com** for more information on The Defining Feature Approach®.

Top tip

Demonstrate the task by creating a couple of musical ideas based on the defining feature yourself, so that students know what you're looking for.

34 Melody recipe

"I love using the melody recipe! It shows me step-by-step how I can write a good tune."

Many students really appreciate a structured approach to composing music. The step-by-step recipe takes them through the process of writing a solid four-bar tune. As with all recipes, there is scope for individual adjustments and creative flair!

This approach is most successful when: it starts with a 'defining feature' (see Idea 33); it is modelled, step-by-step, at the front of the class first; students work at keyboards or preferred instruments, to try out ideas and use the recipe to give structure; students work in even numbers of phrases. Some students may not need to use the recipe but it is handy to refer to as a checklist.

Ingredients

- Choose a key (major/minor).

- Choose a time signature.

- Decide on a pitch direction (up or down).

- Choose a type of movement (triadic, scalic or a combination of the two).

- Start on the tonic.

- The end of bar 2 should finish on the dominant.

- The end of bar 4 should finish on the tonic or dominant.

When students have cooked up their motifs, encourage them to extend and refine them.

Example: short motif based on major third interval

Idea extended and refined:

Developing a melody

"I wrote a really good melody but now I don't know what to do with it!"

Once a student has composed a melody they need to know how to develop it – teaching some solid techniques will move them away from basic repetition and changing the instrument!

The online resources demonstrate the techniques below in a specific example.

○ Invert the melody: There are two ways to invert a melody: strict version (changes the key of the melody), e.g. a descending major third becomes an ascending major third; diatonic version (key remains), e.g. an ascending major third might become a descending minor third.

○ Change the rhythm: Ways to change the rhythm include: adding an anacrusis, syncopation, triplets, dotted rhythm or augmentation/diminution (see below). The addition of some well-placed rests in a melody can also give real impact. Encourage students to explore different types of rest and to play or sing their work to get a feel for the effect.

○ Augmentation and diminution – melodic: Look at the intervals used in the main melody. If you have used a particular interval as a 'defining feature' (see Idea 33), a good way of developing this is to extend or decrease the interval. Gradually augmenting the interval can add excitement and tension.

○ Augmentation and diminution – rhythmic: This is a simple but effective way of altering the rhythm whilst maintaining the pitch. It is also a good way to reinforce teaching of note values.

○ Sequence: Repeat a motif at a higher or lower pitch to extend and develop a melody.

○ Retrograde and inversion: Rewrite the pitches backwards and upside down for a new version of the melody.

○ Chromatically alter notes: To obscure the tonality and add interest, keep the pitches and contour of the melody the same but add a couple of chromatic notes.

Handy hint

Get students to try out these techniques on a pre-existing melody. This way they are not personally attached to the tune and can have a go at using different techniques before moving on to their own composition.

36 Writing a counter-melody

"An effective counter-melody can bring energy and interest to a composition, as well as scope for further development!"

Once students are feeling more confident about writing a melody, the next step could be to write a counter-melody (a secondary tune played alongside the main melody but which should also work in its own right).

First, listen together to some existing examples of successful counter-melodies, for example:

Undine Smith Moore, *Afro-American Suite for Flute, Cello and Piano: Andante* (cello counter-melody when flute enters).

Antonin Dvořák, *Symphony no.8: Movement 3* (strings – with the main theme: about 01:00).

Ennio Morricone, *Gabriel's Oboe* from *The Mission* (strings – second playing of the oboe theme).

Elmer Bernstein, main theme from *The Great Escape* (strings – with woodwind playing the main theme).

Taking it further...

Challenge more able students by asking them to write more than one counter-melody. A great example of this is *One Day More* from the finale of Act I in Les Misérables.

Top tip

Using a DAW or recording facility on a keyboard allows students to try out different counter-melody ideas whilst hearing the main tune and chords at the same time.

Composing a counter-melody

Look at and listen to the main melody and chords. Map out how the second melody might work with the main theme – look for opportunities to use contrary motion, movement in thirds or sixths and more sustained notes over busier sections.

Compose a second melody that fits with the chords.

Adjust the rhythm of the counter-melody so that it complements the main tune – when one melody is active the other should be more static and vice versa.

Record or notate both melodies and chords. Keep listening back and adjusting.

Play the counter-melody on its own to check that it works as an independent line.

Changing background

"I had no idea that so much could be done with the accompaniment!"

This idea explores a technique used by several late 19th-century Russian composers, and encourages A-level and advanced GCSE students to think creatively and explore orchestration.

In 19th-century Russia a group of five composers known as the 'moguchaya kuchka' or 'mighty handful' (Balakirev, Rimsky-Korsakov, Mussorgsky, Borodin and Cui), worked towards creating a Russian nationalist musical style. They were inspired by Glinka's orchestral work, *Kamarinskaya*, which was based on two Russian folk songs (*From beyond the mountains high* and *Kamarinskaya*) and used the compositional technique called 'changing background'. It is exactly as the name describes – a theme is heard repeatedly whilst the supporting background changes – theme and variations in reverse!

In *Kamarinskaya*, the theme is repeated 34 times, with varying orchestral colours and accompaniment. Glinka changes the background in the following ways: adding various counter-melodies; changing the harmony; using different instrumental techniques such as pizzicato; alternating between orchestral sections; creating dissonance through writing pedal notes; passing the main theme round different instruments. Listen to and follow the score of *Kamarinskaya* (see online resources for additional listening pieces; scores may be downloaded free at **imslp.org**). Discuss how the composer has varied the background whilst keeping the theme unchanged.

Give students a theme (example below) and a basic chord outline and ask them to create three or four variations using the changing background technique.

Taking it further...

Add an element of competition: who can write the most variations? Can anyone beat Glinka's 34?

Example

38 Adding chords

"With a logical approach, we can get all students harmonising a simple tune!"

Harmonising a melody is musically satisfying and an important composition skill for students to learn. This idea offers some tips and activity suggestions to use with KS3 and GCSE classes.

Start with three chords (I, IV, V)

The best way to teach chords in the classroom is by playing them. Make it visual and practical by using keyboards, ukuleles, guitars, boomwhackers or voices. Don't be afraid to use the correct technical terms like tonic and dominant from the outset, and be consistent with labelling methods.

At KS3, learn to play a three-chord song, e.g. *Three Little Birds* by Bob Marley or *Somebody that I Used to Know* by Gotye, which demonstrates the use of chords I, IV and V. The 12-bar blues lends itself to learning these chords, with the bonus of introducing added 7th chords and inversions.

Whilst students are learning to play these chords, show them how to construct major and minor triads using the 4 + 3 or 3 + 4 rule.

The 4 + 3 or 3 + 4 rule

This provides a simple method for working out the notes for any root position major or minor triad:

Major triad = 4 + 3 (four semitones followed by three semitones)

Example: C major

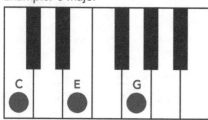

Minor triad = 3 + 4 (three semitones followed by four semitones)

Example: C minor

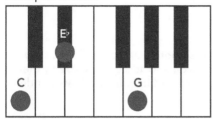

Demonstrating how to harmonise

◉ **Identify the key of the melody**: This can be a good opportunity to cover key signatures up to three sharps/flats.

◉ **Write out chords I, IV and V of the key**.

◉ **Start with the strong beats:** Encourage students to harmonise just the strong beats to start with, e.g. beat 1 or beats 1 and 3 (in 4/4 time).

◉ **Look at the notes of the melody:** Show students how the notes in the melody on the strong beats usually contain one of the notes of the chord to help work out which chord to use.

◉ **Listen and work out by ear when chords need to change:** Play a melody to the students with the first chord sounded. Ask students to listen and suggest where they feel the chord should change.

◉ **Play your chosen chords with the melody to see if they 'work':** Demonstrate this by deliberately choosing some wrong chords to get students hearing the difference.

Inversions

Inversions widen the chord choices available and can make sequences easier and smoother to play. To extend work on adding chords, show how the notes of a triad can be rearranged. This can be visually demonstrated through using boomwhackers, with students physically moving position.

Taking it further...

Once students are confidently using I, IV and V, introduce minor chords ii and vi.

Bonus idea

Give students some melodies with chords added but make sure some are deliberately wrong. Can students work out the wrong chords?

Top tip

For differentiation, use a scaffolding approach (see Idea 47) whereby students are given some of the chords to start with and build up to harmonising a whole phrase on their own.

39 Modulating

"Changing key used to be really scary!"

When a student can change key smoothly and confidently, they demonstrate significant musical skill and add great value to their composition. This idea explores ways of helping students handle modulations at GCSE and A-level.

To change key effectively, knowledge of keys, chords and cadences is required and some preliminary theory work is necessary here. The most common modulations are to related keys: relative major/minor, dominant and subdominant. Help students create a 'key plan' (see example in online resources) to help them simplify their choices.

Give students some example melodies that change key and ask them to identify the start key and the new key. Then, ask students to compose their own melody that includes one modulation, for example:

Students then add chords starting with cadence points. To modulate smoothly, students should use a pivot chord (a chord common to both keys).

Pivot chords

To find a pivot chord, write out the triads for the starting key and the new key (see example online) and circle any chords common to both keys. Then, write them in a table like this:

	Chord: F major	Chord: A minor	Chord: C major	Chord: D minor
F major	I	III	V	vi
C major	IV	Vi	I	ii

Choose one of these chords and check that it fits with the melody. Where possible it is best to choose stronger chords, such as V and I.

Straight after the pivot chord, use a V – I chord progression in the new key. Using a dominant 7th chord usually works well, as the 7th is often foreign to the old key and helps to establish the new key.

Continue in the new key, remembering to add accidentals if necessary.

Model everything! 40

"I find it really helpful when my teacher composes alongside us because I can see what I need to do."

Modelling composing tasks is a key part of building students' confidence levels and providing solid examples that they can follow and develop.

When we teach students to play a keyboard or ukulele piece, demonstrating the song or passage first is a normal part of the activity. Seeing and hearing the teacher play before having a go themselves, is an important part of students' learning. And it's no different when learning to compose – students become more confident when they observe the teacher demonstrating the composing process.

Modelling the composing process

It might seem daunting at first, particularly if you don't consider yourself to be a composer. However, you don't need to compose a symphony off the cuff in front of a class! And, it doesn't have to be perfect. Deliberately (or accidentally) making some mistakes helps students to understand that trying things out and working through errors is all part of the process.

Start by demonstrating how to compose a simple melody. Talk students through the decisions you're making, e.g. "I need to choose a key, so I'm going to go with D major. Then I'm going to decide whether the pitch is going to go up or down…".

Write down the steps you're using on the whiteboard.

Keep it interactive by asking students for feedback: "What could I do to make this bar more interesting?"; "How could I widen the range of this melody?"; and "What happens if I make this a triplet instead of a dotted rhythm?".

Handy hint

To help your own confidence levels, you can work out your ideas in advance, but make it look like you're creating on the spot.

Taking it further...

Try demonstrating how to compose a whole piece or section of a piece – this is particularly helpful if your class is working in the same style. Each lesson, begin by adding a bit more to your composition, giving students a solid example to follow.

41 An integrated approach

"An 'integrated approach': listen — analyse — perform — compose, ensures students are developing all four musical skills in a connected way."

Music is a complex subject comprising the interlinking strands: listening, analysis, performing and composing. Perhaps due to the way in which exam board criteria is presented, these strands are often taught separately and consequently, students can struggle to make connections between them. This idea addresses the issue of 'compartmentalised thinking' and aims to encourage an 'integrated approach' with joined-up thinking.

See online resources for suggested listening pieces with 'tension in music' as a focus.

Top tip

Using an 'integrated approach' doesn't always have to mean putting the activities in the order used here; there may be lessons where you ask students to go straight into a performing or composing task.

Handy hint

Using key words can help to give structure and focus to this type of lesson, e.g. if students are looking at tension in music, key words might include: 'semitone', 'chromaticism', 'tritone'...

Listen

At the start of the lesson, listen to a section of a song or compare a couple of pieces. Ask students to write down a brief description of what they can hear using different headings based on the musical elements.

Analyse

Discuss the ways the composer portrays a particular mood.

Perform

Ask students to play part of the piece you have listened to (e.g. a chord pattern or melody). Through learning to perform it, students are internalising the music and gaining a deeper understanding of the techniques and musical features.

Compose

Create a composition task based around features of the music they have just studied. This could be a small group, paired or individual task. Give students a list of success criteria, to focus the activity (see Idea 43).

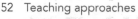

Real-world 42 composing briefs

"My favourite project of the whole year was when we wrote some music for our school 'International week'."

To engage with a task or topic, students often need to see the purpose behind it and understand why they're learning it. Showing how living composers work and giving students a real-life composition brief can be highly motivational and very rewarding – if they know that their music is actually going to be used for something, the whole project takes on a different focus.

Suggestions for real-world composing briefs

◗ Writing a leavers' song for the Year 6 feeder primary school to perform.

◗ Composing a Christmas song to raise money for charity (involves composing, producing and promoting the song).

◗ Composing the background music for a video that the science department is making for the school website.

◗ Year 9 could create a simple percussion piece for Year 7 students to learn in their first term.

◗ Composing a fanfare to be played at the school prize-giving event.

◗ Collaborating with the drama department to compose the incidental music for a play.

Considerations

If this is a new concept in your music department, try introducing a small project to a class which is open to new ideas.

Consider your students: some will baulk at the idea of having their music being played in assembly in front of their peers, but if the project is in small groups, they might be happy to compose a backing track for video, for example.

Not every composing project needs to be run in this way. Perhaps students could build up to a 'real-world' composition task at the end of each year in KS3.

> **Top tip**
>
> Planning is key – make sure there's a clear deadline and arrangements in place for the final performance or recording.

43 Success criteria

"Some clear rubrics keep everyone focussed and on track."

Using success criteria for each composing task, at any stage, is an effective way of keeping students focussed and provides a set of guidelines for assessing the composition and the creative process.

When composing, it is helpful if students can focus on a few key points – it gives a sense of purpose to the activity. For exam groups, success criteria can be derived from the board's mark scheme to keep everyone on track and clear about expectations.

Example composing task

Compose a 60-second introduction to a spy film, using four different instruments. Create suspense and introduce a motif for the main character.

Top tip

Using success criteria can simplify assessing composition: use each criterion as a strand to mark – this way both you and your students are clear on how they achieved the mark and how they could improve.

Handy hint

Refer to the success criteria every lesson to maintain focus, e.g. as a simple starter activity, ask students to choose a criterion to focus on in the lesson and plan how they are going to achieve it.

KS3 example success criteria

❍ Include chromatic movement.

❍ Make use of a pedal note.

❍ Demonstrate understanding of the chosen instruments' capabilities.

❍ Have a clear one- or two-bar motif to be developed later.

GCSE example success criteria

❍ Use at least three melodic development techniques.

❍ Show clear contrast of instrumental texture.

❍ Use musical devices such as pedal and chromaticism to create suspense.

Write the success criteria with the students

Ask students what would make a successful piece and how they could achieve this. This way there is more ownership over the task and the group is likely to be more engaged.

Composing at KS3 44

"I like teaching GCSE composition but at KS3 it's a different ball game."

Teaching composition at KS3 can be challenging, particularly if you have large class sizes, limited space and few or no computers. Whatever your circumstances, it is still possible to get students composing. This idea looks at some options...

There are many ideas presented in this book that can be developed and adapted for your KS3 classes. However as an overview here are five tried and tested approaches:

○ **Graphic score:** Get students listening to a piece of music that lends itself to clear graphical representation. Demonstrate how symbols and a key can depict the music and then get students to create their own composition with graphic score.

○ **Improvising:** This is the best way to get students composing. Give them a set of pitches and an instrument and see what they come up with! A whole-class blues improvisation with backing track is a fun way to get everyone playing their own version of the blues scale.

○ **Body percussion**: Use clicks, claps, hand slides, mouth pops, crossed arm taps and more to get students co-ordinated, moving around and working together as a group. Once they're confident with the movements and corresponding symbols, get them to compose their own body music pieces.

○ **Continue the score:** Give students the start of a composition and ask them to use the given themes to write the next section. This approach allows more confident students to go in their own direction whilst less able students have some ready-made material to work with.

○ **Free composition:** Although it can be tempting to give students parameters for every composing task, it's also important to sometimes provide a stimulus and allow students to create their own music freely.

Taking it further...

Body Beats: An Easy and Fun Guide to the Art of Body Percussion by Ollie Tunmer provides information and guidance, including video materials, on how to use body percussion in the classroom.

45 Composing at GCSE

"How can we get through everything in time?"

Many students find composing a challenging aspect of the GCSE course. Using an 'integrated approach' (see Idea 41) and modelling the compositional process (Idea 40) are helpful in giving students the tools they need to write music. This idea looks at some further ways of supporting our GCSE students...

● **Getting students motivated:** Put together a collection of previous students' compositions or exemplar pieces from exam board training events – they don't all need to be high scorers. Showing these to GCSE students can be a good motivator as they can see what they are aiming for and that it is possible.

● **Portfolio approach:** Setting a number of short technical composing tasks and building up a portfolio before starting coursework, can pay dividends when it comes to student autonomy and confidence levels.

● **In it together:** Some students worry about composing because they feel that they won't be able to do it. Explain that everyone has to start somewhere and that you'll be there to help them. Through modelling composing tasks yourself you will show solidarity with students.

● **Choosing the right brief:** For the set brief you'll need to decide whether you want the whole class working on the same brief or students to choose for themselves. Both approaches can work – it depends on your own expertise, the cohort and your own classroom management style.

● **Mini deadlines:** Breaking down the composition into a series of smaller manageable tasks can seem more achievable and help students keep on-task.

● **Lunchtime composition clinic:** It can be difficult getting round everyone in the class during the lesson. Offering a lunchtime or after-school composition clinic can be time well spent and can help students to progress more quickly.

● **Play to their strengths:** For the free composition, encourage students to write in a style that interests them – they will be far more motivated and engaged.

○ Student-speak mark scheme: To help students understand how their piece is going to be marked, it is a good idea to break down the marking criteria and rephrase it in 'student-speak' so that it is easier to digest.

○ Play engaging examples: Use a diverse range of listening examples that will get your students enthused.

○ Recording work: Leave enough time to make the composition audio recordings. Even if you are exporting from a notation program, over-estimate the time it will take in case there are any technical issues.

○ Plan, plan, plan! Plan the course with composition deadlines in place and share these with students and parents at the outset. Allow yourself plenty of time for marking and moderating to minimise stress levels.

Handy hint

If you're struggling for time, why not enlist the help of some sixth-form students? They could assist GCSE students at lunchtime or after school and help out with performance recordings.

46 Composing at A-level

"Encourage composing that demonstrates flair and imagination..."

Moving from GCSE to A-level can be a huge step up and the bar is undoubtedly much higher for all aspects of the course, not least, composition! This idea gives some inspiration for teaching A-level composition.

○ **Try an 'integrated approach':** An 'integrated approach' (see Idea 41) helps students to make musical connections and link their knowledge from listening and analysing to their composing work.

○ **Use short technical tasks:** Dedicating a number of lessons to exploring various compositional techniques (see previous section) through compiling a portfolio, allows students to practise various skills and gain confidence before embarking on the coursework submission.

○ **Planning the composition:** Students are more focussed when they know where their music is heading, so set aside time for planning and reviewing the composition. Mapping out the structure, key changes and development of ideas, as well as finding examples to listen to, are all helpful tasks at the initial stage.

○ **Flair and imagination:** The main difference between a GCSE and A-level composition (aside from the length) is the level of sophistication expected. Students need to demonstrate a wider range of compositional techniques and show confidence in handling the musical elements (see online resources for examples).

○ **What are the examiners looking for?**

Regardless of the exam board, students need to demonstrate three main things:

○ Composing imaginative themes and motifs.

○ Development of these ideas using a range of techniques within a clear and appropriate structure.

○ Understanding and control of musical elements (melody, harmony, rhythm, etc.).

Top tip

Although it is not a requirement that students submit a live performance of their composition, it is strongly encouraged by the exam boards.

Handy hint

Attend exam board meetings to pick up high-scoring coursework examples in different styles and genres. In addition, Passing Notes Education (**passingnotes education.co.uk**) runs affordable composition webinars and teacher CPD days.

Using scaffolding

"I like it when my teacher gives us some of the chords and we have to fill in the gaps."

Many students benefit from a 'scaffolding' approach to composing tasks. The idea is that students are given the support they need when learning a new technique or skill and become more independent as the support is gradually removed. This idea gives some example ways to use a scaffolding strategy effectively in composing at KS3 or GCSE.

Composing a melody

○ Create a skeleton melody with some notes missing and ask students to fill in the gaps.

○ Give students the first one or two bars of a melody to continue themselves. Ask for four bars first, then build up to an eight-bar melody.

○ Give students a melody bank with two-beat cells to choose from.

○ Give students a one-beat 'rhythm basket' to help construct a two- or four-bar rhythm (see example basket in online resources).

Composing a counter-melody

Give students three different counter-melodies for one main melody with some bars missing for them to complete. Or, provide a simple melodic outline derived from the accompanying chords and ask students to use this as a basis for their own counter-melody.

Adding chords to a melody

Give students a melody with some of the chords filled in. Ask them to choose the remaining chords. Make it more challenging by asking students to include particular types of chord, e.g. inversions or chromatic chords.

Composing a riff

Give students a catchy two-bar rhythm and ask them to add the pitch, or vice versa: give students the pitches and ask them to create the rhythm.

Top tip

Scaffolding is an effective means of differentiating tasks for students.

Bonus idea

A three-tier task system can work well, e.g. labelling tasks as 'warm', 'hot' and 'scorching!' Students choose which tier they will work to with the 'warm' task having the most support and the 'scorching' task requiring students to demonstrate more independence.

48 Feedback and assessment

"A powerful creative act cannot be contained by a neat spreadsheet of numbers and letters." (Robin Hammerton)

How can we effectively assess composition and give feedback in a way that is meaningful and helps students to progress? This is a big question, which cannot be answered in the limited space we have here! However, here are some ideas to get you thinking about assessing composition at KS3 and beyond.

The subjective and creative nature of composing can make it difficult for teachers to assess. Do we evaluate the journey – the techniques and skills explored and developed over time – or just the end product? This is often out of our control. But what is most helpful for the students and time-efficient for you?

A set of rubrics/success criteria (see Idea 43) can be used in conjunction with the following assessment methods.

Assessment radar

Jane Werry's 'Assessment radar' (**werryblog.com**) is a popular choice amongst secondary music teachers. It formatively assesses students, providing comments and feedback, and, depending on your design, can generate a numerical mark at the end. Amend the labels depending on your own assessment criteria. This example for a composition project uses a three-point scale (not yet; can do; can do really well), but you can have five rings instead, labelled 1–5, if requiring a mark.

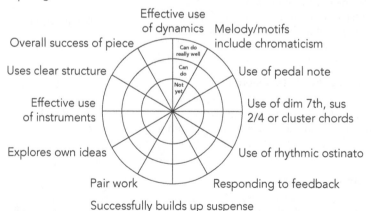

Give each student their own radar sheet and mark a coloured spot on the diagram according to which criteria the student has reached. Use different colours for different dates. Short comments can also be written at the side in the corresponding colour. Remember you don't need to formally assess every composition a student writes!

Verbal feedback

Chatting with students about their work, referring to the success criteria and offering prompts, provides detailed insights to advance their learning.

Peer/self-assessment

Getting students to listen to each others' work and give feedback in relation to success criteria, can boost morale, provide inspiration and allow students to familiarise themselves with evaluation processes.

Student-speak mark schemes

To help students understand coursework assessment criteria, it can be useful to re-write the official mark scheme in 'student-speak' and regularly refer to it.

Handy hint

These two feedback apps are worth checking out:
1. *Showbie* offers a voice recording option, ideal for capturing conversations and feedback to refer to at a later date.
2. *QWIQR Feedback* gives students a QR code to scan to access your verbal feedback.

Taking it further...

Assessment in Music Education by Martin Fautley, and *The National Curriculum for Music – A revised framework for pedagogy and assessment in KS3 Music* by Dr Martin Fautley and Dr Ally Daubney (**ism.org/ images/images/ ISM_The-National-Curriculum-for-Music-booklet_ KS3_2019_digital. pdf**) are well worth a read.

49 Notation software

"Which notation software should I choose? There are so many!"

There are several notation software options available – some are completely free and others come at a cost, though usually with an educational discount. What you choose will depend on your department budget, type of students and personal preference.

Notation software is there to support composing and help students to record their ideas. It is most effective when used in conjunction with creative tasks on instruments or voices.

Notation software

Sibelius: This is a popular program in the classroom. The free version (*Sibelius First*) allows you to write for up to four parts, and includes a cloud-based platform to store up to ten scores. Other versions are now paid for on a monthly/annual subscription.

Dorico: An intuitive and flexible program that allows students to compose without constraint. A free version (*Dorico SE*) is available to try before purchasing the *Elements* or *Pro* versions.

Musescore: This is free and offers an alternative to better-quality programs you need to pay for.

Finale: The free version (Finale NotePad) allows you to write for up to eight staves.

Web-based apps

Noteflight (noteflight.com): This subscription app can work directly with *Soundtrap* enabling students to record their music and see the score in *Noteflight*.

Flat (Flat.io): Integrates with *Google Education*. Not as comprehensive as others, but worth considering for KS3.

Top tip

Attend music education conferences: product specialists demonstrate the programs and you can ask questions. There are often special offers and opportunities to chat to other colleagues too.

Bonus idea

NotePerformer (**noteperformer.com**) has live sampled instrumental sounds for use with *Dorico*, *Sibelius* or *Finale*. A free trial and educational licences are available.

"Digital Audio Workstations can offer wider access to creative music-making for all students."

There are now so many DAWs available that it can be hard to know which to choose and where to start. This idea offers some suggestions, but it is also worth sounding out other music teachers with similar departments.

Some considerations

● **Accessibility for students:** Will they be able to afford the software and engage in creative music-making at home?

● **Industry standard:** Is your software used by the industry? If not, then students will have to learn a new program as they progress.

● **Internet access:** If you are considering a subscription cloud-based program, there will be some limitations, e.g. no video; you and your students will need a reliable internet connection; subscription prices can be increased at any time.

Garageband/Logic: *Garageband* comes as standard on Mac computers, so if you are lucky enough to afford a Mac suite, it is a solid sequencing program to use at KS3 before moving students on to *Logic* at KS4 and KS5.

Cubase: A well-established DAW: *Cubase Elements* can take students through to Cubase Pro as they progress.

Mixcraft: This PC/Mac option is worth considering as an alternative to *GarageBand*.

Ableton Live: Can be used on Mac or PC. It allows the user to control effects, instruments, sounds and other creative features.

Web-based apps
Soundtrap/AudioTool/Soundation/ Hookpad: Entry-level apps which are easy to access (and students can access on their own devices), providing your school has a stable internet connection.

Bandlab: This free cloud-based sequencing app allows student collaboration and teachers to create assignments and give feedback. There is no scoring facility, but work can be exported to any notation program via *MusicXML*.

> **Top tip**
>
> *Musical Futures* and *Ableton* have partnered to produce music technology resources and training for teachers. Find out more at: **musicalfutures. org/mufutv**

Recommended further reading (a selection)

Books

Music Outside the Lines: Ideas for Composing in K-12 Music Classrooms by Maud Hickey (Oxford University Press, 2012)

Assessment in Music Education by Martin Fautley (Oxford University Press, 2010)

How to teach Secondary Music by Hanh Doan and David Guinane (Collins Music, 2017)

Reports/documents

The National Curriculum for Music – A revised framework for pedagogy and assessment in KS3 Music by Dr Martin Fautley and Dr Ally Daubney (ISM, 2019) **ism.org/images/images/ISM_The-National-Curriculum-for-Music-booklet_KS3_2019_digital.pdf**

#CanCompose: National Music Educators Survey by Sound and Music, 2019 **soundandmusic.org/our-impact/can-compose**

Workshops, courses and competitions

The Royal Opera House runs an annual fanfare composing competition and provides online resources for students and teachers: **www.roh.org.uk/learning/young-people/fanfare/teaching-resources**

Sound and Music runs a week-long summer residential for UK composers aged 14–18 years: **soundandmusic.org/learn/summer-school**

Online

Online composition courses and teacher resources: **icancompose.com**

Musical Futures offers a popular approach to song-writing: **musicalfutures.org/resource/songwriting-resource-pack**

How music works series by Howard Goodall (available on **YouTube.com**)

The Listening Project provides daily listening suggestions: (**@listening_16/** on Instagram and Twitter)